# Craft
## NOTES

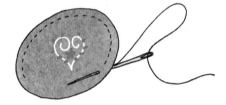

# Craft
## NOTES

**CICO BOOKS**
LONDON  NEW YORK

Published in 2014 by CICO Books
an imprint of Ryland Peters & Small Ltd
20–21 Jockey's Fields, London WC1R 4BW
519 Broadway, 5th Floor, New York, NY 10012

www.rylandpeters.com

10 9 8 7 6 5 4 3 2 1

Compilation © CICO Books 2014

Design © CICO Books 2014

Illustration on jacket © CORBIS
Illustrations on pages 2–4, 9–39, 41, 73–101, 103–137 © CORBIS
All other illustrations © CICO Books

A CIP catalog record for this book is available from the Library of
Congress and the British Library.

ISBN: 978-1-78249-114-9

Designer: Emily Breen

Printed in China

# Contents

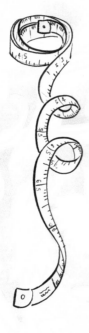

# Introduction

The pace of modern life can make it hard to find time to be creative, and to experience the pleasure of making things with your own hands. But every crafter knows the immense sense of pride and satisfaction that comes from creating a perfectly-fitting dress, knitting a Fair Isle sweater, or making your own greeting cards.

Whatever your favorite craft, it is useful to have somewhere to jot down ideas and inspirations, sketch out designs, and record the details—and the results—of your projects. *Craft Notes* provides you with the perfect place to keep track of everything you have made, and everything you want to make.

Use the moodboards to paste in cuttings from magazines and newspapers, samples of fabric and yarn, photographs, textures, and anything else that inspires you. There is also a useful envelope at the back of the journal, in which you can keep fabric and yarn labels, shade charts, and anything else that catches your eye.

The section of pages printed with grids is perfect for sketching out patterns and laying out motifs, such as cross-stitch or intarsia designs.

Three sections of project records, for Sewing, Knitting and Crochet, and Other Crafts, all provide ample space for you to note down the details of your own makes, so you will always be able to remember exactly what yarn you used, or how much fabric was really required for a particular sewing pattern. There is also space for you to paste in a picture of the finished item—particularly useful when you have given it as a gift, and then want to make another! You can even record who you gave it to, and make notes of your own on what you learned, and how the project turned out.

Finally, there is space for you to note down your favorite resources—websites, blogs, magazines, and perhaps the phone numbers of your local suppliers, or contact addresses for craft groups.

So make sure that your projects are recorded and that you keep organized with this journal, and you will have more time for what matters most to you—making!

# Inspiration
## and Ideas

# Moodboard

# Moodboard

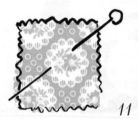

# Moodboard

# Moodboard

# Moodboard

# Moodboard

# Moodboard

# Moodboard

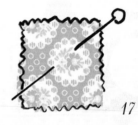

# Moodboard

# Moodboard

# Moodboard

# Moodboard

# Moodboard

# Moodboard

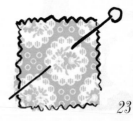

# Sketches

# Sketches

# Sketches

# Sketches

# Sketches

# Sketches

# Sketches

# Sketches

# Sketches

# Sketches

# Sketches

# Sketches

# Sketches

# Sketches

# Sketches

# Sketches

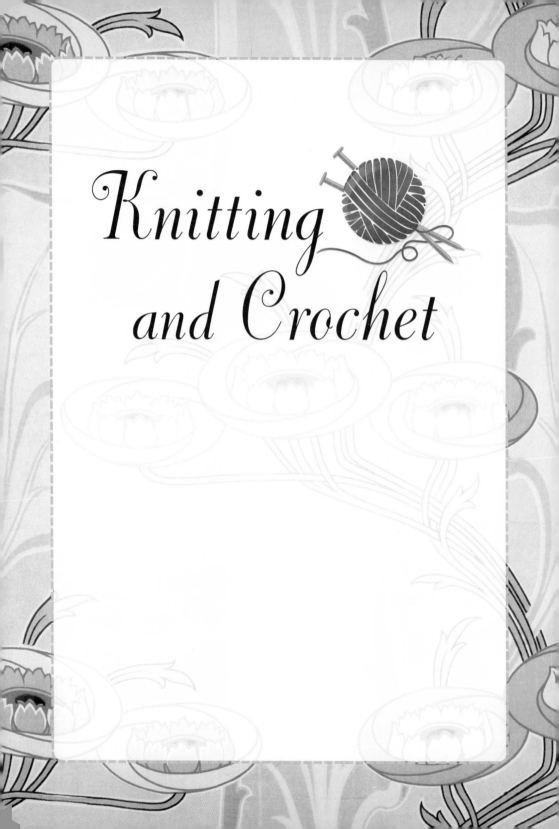

# Knitting and Crochet

# Knitting or Crochet Project

Name:
..............................................................

Date begun:
..............................................................

Date completed:
..............................................................

Who I made it for:
..............................................................

Pattern source:
..............................................................
..............................................................

Needle/hook size used:
..............................................................

Yarn type used:
..............................................................

Color/dye lot number:
..............................................................

Yarn quantity used:
..............................................................

Washing instructions:
..............................................................
..............................................................
..............................................................
..............................................................

*Attach photograph of project here*

My notes:
..............................................................
..............................................................
..............................................................
..............................................................
..............................................................
..............................................................
..............................................................
..............................................................
..............................................................
..............................................................
..............................................................
..............................................................
..............................................................
..............................................................
..............................................................
..............................................................
..............................................................
..............................................................
..............................................................
..............................................................
..............................................................
..............................................................
..............................................................

# Knitting or Crochet Project

Name:

Date begun:

Date completed:

Who I made it for:

Pattern source:

Needle/hook size used:

Yarn type used:

Color/dye lot number:

Yarn quantity used:

Washing instructions:

*Attach photograph of project here*

My notes:

# Knitting or Crochet Project

Name: ...................................................

Date begun: ...........................................

Date completed: ......................................

Who I made it for: ...................................

Pattern source: .......................................

.............................................................

Needle/hook size used: ............................

Yarn type used: ......................................

Color/dye lot number: .............................

Yarn quantity used: .................................

Washing instructions: ..............................

.............................................................

.............................................................

.............................................................

.............................................................

My notes: .................................................

.............................................................

.............................................................

.............................................................

.............................................................

.............................................................

.............................................................

.............................................................

.............................................................

.............................................................

.............................................................

.............................................................

.............................................................

.............................................................

.............................................................

.............................................................

.............................................................

.............................................................

.............................................................

.............................................................

.............................................................

.............................................................

.............................................................

*Attach photograph of project here*

# Knitting or Crochet Project

Name: ......................................................

Date begun: ..............................................

Date completed: .........................................

Who I made it for: .......................................

Pattern source: ..........................................

......................................................................

Needle/hook size used: .................................

Yarn type used: ..........................................

Color/dye lot number: ..................................

Yarn quantity used: .....................................

Washing instructions: ..................................

......................................................................

......................................................................

......................................................................

......................................................................

*Attach photograph of project here*

My notes: ...............................................

......................................................................

......................................................................

......................................................................

......................................................................

......................................................................

......................................................................

......................................................................

......................................................................

......................................................................

......................................................................

......................................................................

......................................................................

......................................................................

......................................................................

......................................................................

......................................................................

......................................................................

......................................................................

......................................................................

......................................................................

......................................................................

......................................................................

......................................................................

......................................................................

# Knitting or Crochet Project

Name: ....................................................

Date begun: ..............................................

Date completed: ..........................................

Who I made it for: .......................................

Pattern source: ..........................................

...........................................................

Needle/hook size used: ...................................

Yarn type used: ..........................................

Color/dye lot number: ....................................

Yarn quantity used: ......................................

Washing instructions: ....................................

...........................................................

...........................................................

...........................................................

...........................................................

*Attach photograph of project here*

My notes: ................................................

...........................................................

...........................................................

...........................................................

...........................................................

...........................................................

...........................................................

...........................................................

...........................................................

...........................................................

...........................................................

...........................................................

...........................................................

...........................................................

...........................................................

...........................................................

...........................................................

...........................................................

...........................................................

...........................................................

...........................................................

# Knitting or Crochet Project

Name:

Date begun:

Date completed:

Who I made it for:

Pattern source:

Needle/hook size used:

Yarn type used:

Color/dye lot number:

Yarn quantity used:

Washing instructions:

My notes:

*Attach photograph of project here*

# Knitting or Crochet Project

Name: .....................................................

Date begun: ...........................................

Date completed: ....................................

Who I made it for: ................................

Pattern source: .....................................

.................................................................

Needle/hook size used: .....................

Yarn type used: ....................................

Color/dye lot number: .....................

Yarn quantity used: ...........................

Washing instructions: .......................

.................................................................

.................................................................

.................................................................

.................................................................

My notes: .................................................

.................................................................

.................................................................

.................................................................

.................................................................

.................................................................

.................................................................

.................................................................

.................................................................

.................................................................

.................................................................

.................................................................

.................................................................

.................................................................

.................................................................

.................................................................

.................................................................

.................................................................

.................................................................

.................................................................

.................................................................

.................................................................

.................................................................

.................................................................

*Attach photograph of project here*

# Knitting or Crochet Project

Name:

Date begun:

Date completed:

Who I made it for:

Pattern source:

Needle/hook size used:

Yarn type used:

Color/dye lot number:

Yarn quantity used:

Washing instructions:

*Attach photograph of project here*

My notes:

# Knitting or Crochet Project

Name:

Date begun:

Date completed:

Who I made it for:

Pattern source:

Needle/hook size used:

Yarn type used:

Color/dye lot number:

Yarn quantity used:

Washing instructions:

My notes:

*Attach photograph of project here*

# Knitting or Crochet Project

Name:

Date begun:

Date completed:

Who I made it for:

Pattern source:

Needle/hook size used:

Yarn type used:

Color/dye lot number:

Yarn quantity used:

Washing instructions:

*Attach photograph of project here*

My notes:

# Knitting or Crochet Project

Name: ......................................................

Date begun: ...............................................

Date completed: ..........................................

Who I made it for: .......................................

Pattern source: ...........................................

......................................................

Needle/hook size used: .................................

Yarn type used: ...........................................

Color/dye lot number: ..................................

Yarn quantity used: ......................................

Washing instructions: ...................................

......................................................

......................................................

......................................................

*Attach photograph of project here*

My notes: ...............................................

......................................................

......................................................

......................................................

......................................................

......................................................

......................................................

......................................................

......................................................

......................................................

......................................................

......................................................

......................................................

......................................................

......................................................

......................................................

......................................................

......................................................

......................................................

# Knitting or Crochet Project

Name:

Date begun:

Date completed:

Who I made it for:

Pattern source:

Needle/hook size used:

Yarn type used:

Color/dye lot number:

Yarn quantity used:

Washing instructions:

*Attach photograph of project here*

My notes:

# Knitting or Crochet Project

Name:
.............................................

Date begun:
.............................................

Date completed:
.............................................

Who I made it for:
.............................................

Pattern source:
.............................................
.............................................

Needle/hook size used:
.............................................

Yarn type used:
.............................................

Color/dye lot number:
.............................................

Yarn quantity used:
.............................................

Washing instructions:
.............................................
.............................................
.............................................
.............................................

*Attach photograph of project here*

My notes:
.............................................
.............................................
.............................................
.............................................
.............................................
.............................................
.............................................
.............................................
.............................................
.............................................
.............................................
.............................................
.............................................
.............................................
.............................................
.............................................
.............................................
.............................................
.............................................
.............................................
.............................................
.............................................
.............................................

# Knitting or Crochet Project

Name:

Date begun:

Date completed:

Who I made it for:

Pattern source:

Needle/hook size used:

Yarn type used:

Color/dye lot number:

Yarn quantity used:

Washing instructions:

*Attach photograph of project here*

My notes:

# Knitting or Crochet Project

Name: .......................................................

Date begun: ............................................

Date completed: ....................................

Who I made it for: ...............................

Pattern source: ......................................
..................................................................

Needle/hook size used: .......................

Yarn type used: ......................................

Color/dye lot number: .........................

Yarn quantity used: ..............................

Washing instructions: ..........................
..................................................................
..................................................................
..................................................................
..................................................................

My notes: ........................................................
.....................................................................
.....................................................................
.....................................................................
.....................................................................
.....................................................................
.....................................................................
.....................................................................
.....................................................................
.....................................................................
.....................................................................
.....................................................................
.....................................................................
.....................................................................
.....................................................................
.....................................................................
.....................................................................
.....................................................................
.....................................................................
.....................................................................
.....................................................................
.....................................................................
.....................................................................

*Attach photograph of project here*

# Knitting or Crochet Project

Name:

Date begun:

Date completed:

Who I made it for:

Pattern source:

Needle/hook size used:

Yarn type used:

Color/dye lot number:

Yarn quantity used:

Washing instructions:

*Attach photograph of project here*

My notes:

# Knitting or Crochet Project

Name:
......................................................

Date begun:
......................................................

Date completed:
......................................................

Who I made it for:
......................................................

Pattern source:
......................................................
......................................................

Needle/hook size used:
......................................................

Yarn type used:
......................................................

Color/dye lot number:
......................................................

Yarn quantity used:
......................................................

Washing instructions:
......................................................
......................................................
......................................................
......................................................
......................................................

My notes:
......................................................
......................................................
......................................................
......................................................
......................................................
......................................................
......................................................
......................................................
......................................................
......................................................
......................................................
......................................................
......................................................
......................................................
......................................................
......................................................
......................................................
......................................................
......................................................
......................................................

*Attach photograph of project here*

# Knitting or Crochet Project

Name:
.................................................................

Date begun:
.................................................................

Date completed:
.................................................................

Who I made it for:
.................................................................

Pattern source:
.................................................................
.................................................................

Needle/hook size used:
.................................................................

Yarn type used:
.................................................................

Color/dye lot number:
.................................................................

Yarn quantity used:
.................................................................

Washing instructions:
.................................................................
.................................................................
.................................................................
.................................................................
.................................................................

*Attach photograph of project here*

My notes:
.................................................................
.................................................................
.................................................................
.................................................................
.................................................................
.................................................................
.................................................................
.................................................................
.................................................................
.................................................................
.................................................................
.................................................................
.................................................................
.................................................................
.................................................................
.................................................................
.................................................................
.................................................................
.................................................................
.................................................................
.................................................................
.................................................................
.................................................................
.................................................................
.................................................................
.................................................................

# Knitting or Crochet Project

Name: .....................................................

Date begun: ...........................................

Date completed: .....................................

Who I made it for: ...............................

Pattern source: .....................................
...........................................................

Needle/hook size used: .......................

Yarn type used: ....................................

Color/dye lot number: .........................

Yarn quantity used: .............................

Washing instructions: ..........................
...........................................................
...........................................................
...........................................................
...........................................................

*Attach photograph of project here*

My notes: ..............................................
...........................................................
...........................................................
...........................................................
...........................................................
...........................................................
...........................................................
...........................................................
...........................................................
...........................................................
...........................................................
...........................................................
...........................................................
...........................................................
...........................................................
...........................................................
...........................................................
...........................................................
...........................................................
...........................................................
...........................................................
...........................................................
...........................................................
...........................................................

# Knitting or Crochet Project

Name: ........................................

Date begun: ........................................

Date completed: ........................................

Who I made it for: ........................................

Pattern source: ........................................

........................................

Needle/hook size used: ........................................

Yarn type used: ........................................

Color/dye lot number: ........................................

Yarn quantity used: ........................................

Washing instructions: ........................................

........................................

........................................

........................................

My notes: ........................................

........................................

........................................

........................................

........................................

........................................

........................................

........................................

........................................

........................................

........................................

........................................

........................................

........................................

........................................

........................................

........................................

........................................

........................................

........................................

........................................

........................................

*Attach photograph of project here*

# Knitting or Crochet Project

Name: .....................................................

Date begun: .............................................

Date completed: .......................................

Who I made it for: ...................................

Pattern source: ........................................

...................................................................

Needle/hook size used: ...........................

Yarn type used: ........................................

Color/dye lot number: .............................

Yarn quantity used: .................................

Washing instructions: .............................

...................................................................

...................................................................

...................................................................

My notes: ...................................................

...................................................................

...................................................................

...................................................................

...................................................................

...................................................................

...................................................................

...................................................................

...................................................................

...................................................................

...................................................................

...................................................................

...................................................................

...................................................................

...................................................................

...................................................................

...................................................................

...................................................................

...................................................................

*Attach photograph of project here*

# Knitting or Crochet Project

Name: ......................................................

Date begun: ..............................................

Date completed: ........................................

Who I made it for: ....................................

Pattern source: .........................................

..................................................................

Needle/hook size used: .............................

Yarn type used: .........................................

Color/dye lot number: ...............................

Yarn quantity used: ...................................

Washing instructions: ................................

..................................................................

..................................................................

..................................................................

..................................................................

*Attach photograph of project here*

My notes: ...................................................

..................................................................
..................................................................
..................................................................
..................................................................
..................................................................
..................................................................
..................................................................
..................................................................
..................................................................
..................................................................
..................................................................
..................................................................
..................................................................
..................................................................
..................................................................
..................................................................
..................................................................
..................................................................
..................................................................
..................................................................
..................................................................
..................................................................
..................................................................
..................................................................

# Knitting or Crochet Project

Name: ..........................................

Date begun: ..................................

Date completed: .............................

Who I made it for: ..........................

Pattern source: ..............................

..................................................

Needle/hook size used: ....................

Yarn type used: ..............................

Color/dye lot number: .....................

Yarn quantity used: .........................

Washing instructions: ......................

..................................................

..................................................

..................................................

..................................................

My notes: ......................................

..................................................

..................................................

..................................................

..................................................

..................................................

..................................................

..................................................

..................................................

..................................................

..................................................

..................................................

..................................................

..................................................

..................................................

..................................................

..................................................

..................................................

..................................................

..................................................

..................................................

..................................................

*Attach photograph of project here*

# Knitting or Crochet Project

Name: .........................................................

Date begun: .................................................

Date completed: ...........................................

Who I made it for: .......................................

Pattern source: ............................................

.........................................................................

Needle/hook size used: ...............................

Yarn type used: ...........................................

Color/dye lot number: .................................

Yarn quantity used: .....................................

Washing instructions: ..................................

.........................................................................

.........................................................................

.........................................................................

.........................................................................

*Attach photograph of project here*

My notes: ....................................................

.........................................................................

.........................................................................

.........................................................................

.........................................................................

.........................................................................

.........................................................................

.........................................................................

.........................................................................

.........................................................................

.........................................................................

.........................................................................

.........................................................................

.........................................................................

.........................................................................

.........................................................................

.........................................................................

.........................................................................

.........................................................................

.........................................................................

.........................................................................

.........................................................................

# Knitting or Crochet Project

Name: .........................................................

Date begun: ...............................................

Date completed: .........................................

Who I made it for: ....................................

Pattern source: ..........................................

.........................................................................

Needle/hook size used: ...........................

Yarn type used: .........................................

Color/dye lot number: .............................

Yarn quantity used: ..................................

Washing instructions: ..............................

.........................................................................

.........................................................................

.........................................................................

My notes: ...................................................

.........................................................................

.........................................................................

.........................................................................

.........................................................................

.........................................................................

.........................................................................

.........................................................................

.........................................................................

.........................................................................

.........................................................................

.........................................................................

.........................................................................

.........................................................................

.........................................................................

.........................................................................

.........................................................................

.........................................................................

.........................................................................

.........................................................................

*Attach photograph of project here*

# Knitting or Crochet Project

Name:

Date begun:

Date completed:

Who I made it for:

Pattern source:

Needle/hook size used:

Yarn type used:

Color/dye lot number:

Yarn quantity used:

Washing instructions:

My notes:

*Attach photograph of project here*

# Knitting or Crochet Project

Name:

Date begun:

Date completed:

Who I made it for:

Pattern source:

Needle/hook size used:

Yarn type used:

Color/dye lot number:

Yarn quantity used:

Washing instructions:

My notes:

*Attach photograph of project here*

# Knitting or Crochet Project

Name:
.............................................................

Date begun:
.............................................................

Date completed:
.............................................................

Who I made it for:
.............................................................

Pattern source:
.............................................................

.............................................................

Needle/hook size used:
.............................................................

Yarn type used:
.............................................................

Color/dye lot number:
.............................................................

Yarn quantity used:
.............................................................

Washing instructions:
.............................................................

.............................................................

.............................................................

.............................................................

.............................................................

*Attach photograph of project here*

My notes:
.............................................................
.............................................................
.............................................................
.............................................................
.............................................................
.............................................................
.............................................................
.............................................................
.............................................................
.............................................................
.............................................................
.............................................................
.............................................................
.............................................................
.............................................................
.............................................................
.............................................................
.............................................................
.............................................................
.............................................................
.............................................................
.............................................................
.............................................................
.............................................................

# Knitting or Crochet Project

Name:
.................................................

Date begun:
.................................................

Date completed:
.................................................

Who I made it for:
.................................................

Pattern source:
.................................................

.................................................

Needle/hook size used:
.................................................

Yarn type used:
.................................................

Color/dye lot number:
.................................................

Yarn quantity used:
.................................................

Washing instructions:
.................................................

.................................................

.................................................

.................................................

My notes:
.................................................
.................................................
.................................................
.................................................
.................................................
.................................................
.................................................
.................................................
.................................................
.................................................
.................................................
.................................................
.................................................
.................................................
.................................................
.................................................
.................................................
.................................................
.................................................
.................................................
.................................................
.................................................
.................................................
.................................................
.................................................
.................................................

*Attach photograph of project here*

# Knitting or Crochet Project

Name: .............................................

Date begun: .....................................

Date completed: ...............................

Who I made it for: ............................

Pattern source: .................................

.............................................................

Needle/hook size used: ....................

Yarn type used: ................................

Color/dye lot number: ......................

Yarn quantity used: ..........................

Washing instructions: .......................

.............................................................

.............................................................

.............................................................

.............................................................

*Attach photograph of project here*

My notes: .........................................

.............................................................

.............................................................

.............................................................

.............................................................

.............................................................

.............................................................

.............................................................

.............................................................

.............................................................

.............................................................

.............................................................

.............................................................

.............................................................

.............................................................

.............................................................

.............................................................

.............................................................

.............................................................

.............................................................

.............................................................

.............................................................

.............................................................

# Sewing

# Sewing Project

Name:

Date begun:

Date completed:

Pattern source:

Fabric used:

Fabric quantity used:

My notes:

*Attach photograph of project here*

# Sewing Project

Name:

Date begun:

Date completed:

Pattern source:

Fabric used:

Fabric quantity used:

*Attach photograph of project here*

My notes:

# Sewing Project

Name:
.....................................................

Date begun:
.....................................................

Date completed:
.....................................................

Pattern source:
.....................................................
.....................................................

Fabric used:

Fabric quantity used:
.....................................................
.....................................................
.....................................................
.....................................................
.....................................................
.....................................................
.....................................................
.....................................................

*Attach photograph of project here*

My notes:
.....................................................
.....................................................
.....................................................
.....................................................
.....................................................
.....................................................
.....................................................
.....................................................
.....................................................
.....................................................
.....................................................
.....................................................
.....................................................
.....................................................
.....................................................
.....................................................
.....................................................
.....................................................
.....................................................
.....................................................
.....................................................

# Sewing Project

Name:

Date begun:

Date completed:

Pattern source:

Fabric used:

Fabric quantity used:

*Attach photograph of project here*

My notes:

# Sewing Project

Name: ..................................................

Date begun: ..........................................

Date completed: .....................................

Pattern source: ......................................

..................................................

Fabric used: .........................................

Fabric quantity used: ..............................

..................................................

..................................................

..................................................

..................................................

..................................................

My notes: ............................................

..................................................

..................................................

..................................................

..................................................

..................................................

..................................................

..................................................

..................................................

..................................................

..................................................

..................................................

..................................................

..................................................

..................................................

..................................................

..................................................

..................................................

..................................................

..................................................

..................................................

*Attach photograph of project here*

# Sewing Project

Name: ......................................

Date begun: ..............................

Date completed: ..........................

Pattern source: ...........................

...............................................

Fabric used: ...............................

Fabric quantity used: ....................

...............................................

...............................................

...............................................

...............................................

...............................................

...............................................

*Attach photograph of project here*

My notes: ...........................................

...........................................................

...........................................................

...........................................................

...........................................................

...........................................................

...........................................................

...........................................................

...........................................................

...........................................................

...........................................................

...........................................................

...........................................................

...........................................................

...........................................................

...........................................................

...........................................................

...........................................................

...........................................................

...........................................................

...........................................................

# Sewing Project

Name:

Date begun:

Date completed:

Pattern source:

Fabric used:

Fabric quantity used:

My notes:

*Attach photograph of project here*

# Sewing Project

Name: ..................................................

Date begun: ..........................................

Date completed: ....................................

Pattern source: .....................................

..........................................................

Fabric used: ..........................................

Fabric quantity used: ..............................

..........................................................

..........................................................

..........................................................

..........................................................

..........................................................

..........................................................

*Attach photograph of project here*

My notes: .............................................

..........................................................

..........................................................

..........................................................

..........................................................

..........................................................

..........................................................

..........................................................

..........................................................

..........................................................

..........................................................

..........................................................

..........................................................

..........................................................

..........................................................

..........................................................

..........................................................

..........................................................

..........................................................

..........................................................

..........................................................

..........................................................

# Sewing Project

Name:

Date begun:

Date completed:

Pattern source:

Fabric used:

Fabric quantity used:

My notes:

*Attach photograph of project here*

# Sewing Project

Name:
.................................................

Date begun:
.................................................

Date completed:
.................................................

Pattern source:
.................................................
.................................................

Fabric used:
.................................................

Fabric quantity used:
.................................................
.................................................
.................................................
.................................................
.................................................
.................................................
.................................................
.................................................

*Attach photograph of project here*

My notes:
.................................................
.................................................
.................................................
.................................................
.................................................
.................................................
.................................................
.................................................
.................................................
.................................................
.................................................
.................................................
.................................................
.................................................
.................................................
.................................................
.................................................
.................................................
.................................................
.................................................
.................................................
.................................................

# Sewing Project

Name:

Date begun:

Date completed:

Pattern source:

Fabric used:

Fabric quantity used:

My notes:

*Attach photograph of project here*

# Sewing Project

Name:
.............................................

Date begun:
.............................................

Date completed:
.............................................

Pattern source:
.............................................
.............................................

Fabric used:
.............................................

Fabric quantity used:
.............................................
.............................................
.............................................
.............................................
.............................................
.............................................
.............................................

*Attach photograph of project here*

My notes:
.............................................
.............................................
.............................................
.............................................
.............................................
.............................................
.............................................
.............................................
.............................................
.............................................
.............................................
.............................................
.............................................
.............................................
.............................................
.............................................
.............................................
.............................................
.............................................
.............................................
.............................................
.............................................
.............................................
.............................................

# Sewing Project

Name:
................................

Date begun:
................................

Date completed:
................................

Pattern source:
................................
................................

Fabric used:
................................

Fabric quantity used:
................................
................................
................................
................................
................................
................................

My notes:
................................
................................
................................
................................
................................
................................
................................
................................
................................
................................
................................
................................
................................
................................
................................
................................
................................
................................
................................
................................
................................
................................

*Attach photograph of project here*

# Sewing Project

Name:

Date begun:

Date completed:

Pattern source:


Fabric used:

Fabric quantity used:

My notes:

*Attach photograph of project here*

# Sewing Project

Name:
..................................................................

Date begun:
..................................................................

Date completed:
..................................................................

Pattern source:
..................................................................

..................................................................

Fabric used:
..................................................................

Fabric quantity used:
..................................................................

..................................................................

..................................................................

..................................................................

..................................................................

..................................................................

..................................................................

*Attach photograph of project here*

My notes:
..................................................................
..................................................................
..................................................................
..................................................................
..................................................................
..................................................................
..................................................................
..................................................................
..................................................................
..................................................................
..................................................................
..................................................................
..................................................................
..................................................................
..................................................................
..................................................................
..................................................................
..................................................................
..................................................................
..................................................................
..................................................................
..................................................................
..................................................................
..................................................................
..................................................................

# Sewing Project

Name:
.....................................................

Date begun:
.....................................................

Date completed:
.....................................................

Pattern source:
.....................................................
.....................................................

Fabric used:
.....................................................

Fabric quantity used:
.....................................................
.....................................................
.....................................................
.....................................................
.....................................................
.....................................................

My notes:
.....................................................
.....................................................
.....................................................
.....................................................
.....................................................
.....................................................
.....................................................
.....................................................
.....................................................
.....................................................
.....................................................
.....................................................
.....................................................
.....................................................
.....................................................
.....................................................
.....................................................
.....................................................
.....................................................
.....................................................
.....................................................
.....................................................
.....................................................
.....................................................

*Attach photograph of project here*

# Sewing Project

Name:

Date begun:

Date completed:

Pattern source:

Fabric used:

Fabric quantity used:

My notes:

*Attach photograph of project here*

# Sewing Project

Name: ..............................

Date begun: ..............................

Date completed: ..............................

Pattern source: ..............................

..............................

Fabric used: ..............................

Fabric quantity used: ..............................

..............................

..............................

..............................

..............................

..............................

..............................

..............................

*Attach photograph of project here*

My notes: ..............................

..............................

..............................

..............................

..............................

..............................

..............................

..............................

..............................

..............................

..............................

..............................

..............................

..............................

..............................

..............................

..............................

..............................

..............................

..............................

..............................

..............................

..............................

# Sewing Project

Name:

Date begun:

Date completed:

Pattern source:

Fabric used:

Fabric quantity used:

My notes:

*Attach photograph of project here*

# Sewing Project

Name:

Date begun:

Date completed:

Pattern source:

Fabric used:

Fabric quantity used:

My notes:

*Attach photograph of project here*

# Sewing Project

Name:
.......................................................

Date begun:
.......................................................

Date completed:
.......................................................

Pattern source:
.......................................................
.......................................................

Fabric used:
.......................................................

Fabric quantity used:
.......................................................
.......................................................
.......................................................
.......................................................
.......................................................
.......................................................

My notes:
.......................................................
.......................................................
.......................................................
.......................................................
.......................................................
.......................................................
.......................................................
.......................................................
.......................................................
.......................................................
.......................................................
.......................................................
.......................................................
.......................................................
.......................................................
.......................................................
.......................................................

*Attach photograph of project here*

# Sewing Project

Name:

Date begun:

Date completed:

Pattern source:

Fabric used:

Fabric quantity used:

My notes:

*Attach photograph of project here*

# Sewing Project

Name:
.........................................

Date begun:
.........................................

Date completed:
.........................................

Pattern source:
.........................................
.........................................

Fabric used:
.........................................

Fabric quantity used:
.........................................
.........................................
.........................................
.........................................
.........................................
.........................................
.........................................

*Attach photograph of project here*

My notes:
.........................................
.........................................
.........................................
.........................................
.........................................
.........................................
.........................................
.........................................
.........................................
.........................................
.........................................
.........................................
.........................................
.........................................
.........................................
.........................................
.........................................
.........................................
.........................................
.........................................
.........................................
.........................................
.........................................
.........................................
.........................................
.........................................

# Sewing Project

Name:
..................................................

Date begun:
..................................................

Date completed:
..................................................

Pattern source:
..................................................
..................................................

Fabric used:
..................................................

Fabric quantity used:
..................................................
..................................................
..................................................
..................................................
..................................................
..................................................
..................................................

My notes:
..................................................
..................................................
..................................................
..................................................
..................................................
..................................................
..................................................
..................................................
..................................................
..................................................
..................................................
..................................................
..................................................
..................................................
..................................................
..................................................
..................................................
..................................................
..................................................
..................................................
..................................................
..................................................

*Attach photograph of project here*

97

# Sewing Project

Name:

Date begun:

Date completed:

Pattern source:

Fabric used:

Fabric quantity used:

My notes:

*Attach photograph of project here*

# Sewing Project

Name:
........................................................

Date begun:
........................................................

Date completed:
........................................................

Pattern source:
........................................................
........................................................

Fabric used:
........................................................

Fabric quantity used:
........................................................
........................................................
........................................................
........................................................
........................................................
........................................................

*Attach photograph of project here*

My notes:
........................................................
........................................................
........................................................
........................................................
........................................................
........................................................
........................................................
........................................................
........................................................
........................................................
........................................................
........................................................
........................................................
........................................................
........................................................
........................................................
........................................................
........................................................
........................................................
........................................................
........................................................
........................................................
........................................................

# Sewing Project

Name:

Date begun:

Date completed:

Pattern source:

Fabric used:

Fabric quantity used:

My notes:

*Attach photograph of project here*

# Sewing Project

Name:

Date begun:

Date completed:

Pattern source:

Fabric used:

Fabric quantity used:

My notes:

*Attach photograph of project here*

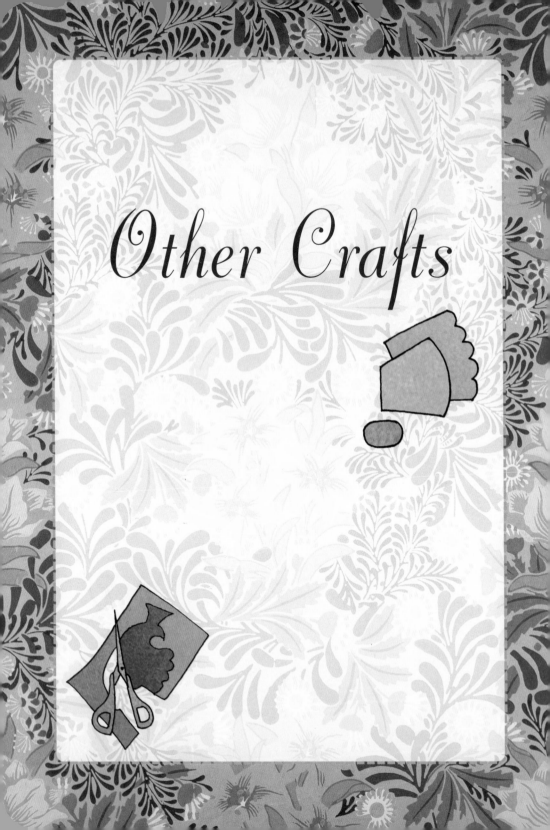

# Other Crafts

# Craft Project

Name:
..............................................................

Date begun:
..............................................................

Date completed:
..............................................................

Who I made it for:
..............................................................

Inspiration or pattern source:
..............................................................
..............................................................

Materials used:
..............................................................
..............................................................
..............................................................
..............................................................
..............................................................
..............................................................

My notes:
..............................................................
..............................................................
..............................................................
..............................................................
..............................................................
..............................................................
..............................................................
..............................................................
..............................................................
..............................................................
..............................................................
..............................................................
..............................................................
..............................................................
..............................................................
..............................................................
..............................................................
..............................................................
..............................................................

*Attach photograph of project here*

# Craft Project

Name: ....................................................

Date begun: ............................................

Date completed: ......................................

Who I made it for: ..................................

Inspiration or pattern source: ...............
....................................................................

Materials used: ......................................
....................................................................
....................................................................
....................................................................
....................................................................
....................................................................
....................................................................

*Attach photograph of project here*

My notes: ................................................
....................................................................
....................................................................
....................................................................
....................................................................
....................................................................
....................................................................
....................................................................
....................................................................
....................................................................
....................................................................
....................................................................
....................................................................
....................................................................
....................................................................
....................................................................
....................................................................
....................................................................
....................................................................
....................................................................
....................................................................
....................................................................
....................................................................

# Craft Project

Name:
.................................................

Date begun:
.................................................

Date completed:
.................................................

Who I made it for:
.................................................

Inspiration or pattern source:
.................................................
.................................................

Materials used:
.................................................
.................................................
.................................................
.................................................
.................................................
.................................................
.................................................

*Attach photograph of project here*

My notes:
.................................................
.................................................
.................................................
.................................................
.................................................
.................................................
.................................................
.................................................
.................................................
.................................................
.................................................
.................................................
.................................................
.................................................
.................................................
.................................................
.................................................
.................................................
.................................................
.................................................
.................................................

# Craft Project

Name:

Date begun:

Date completed:

Who I made it for:

Inspiration or pattern source:

Materials used:

*Attach photograph of project here*

My notes:

# Craft Project

Name:

Date begun:

Date completed:

Who I made it for:

Inspiration or pattern source:

Materials used:

My notes:

Attach photograph of project here

# Craft Project

Name:
.........................................................................

Date begun:
.........................................................................

Date completed:
.........................................................................

Who I made it for:
.........................................................................

Inspiration or pattern source:
.........................................................................
.........................................................................

Materials used:
.........................................................................
.........................................................................
.........................................................................
.........................................................................
.........................................................................
.........................................................................
.........................................................................

My notes:
.........................................................................
.........................................................................
.........................................................................
.........................................................................
.........................................................................
.........................................................................
.........................................................................
.........................................................................
.........................................................................
.........................................................................
.........................................................................
.........................................................................
.........................................................................
.........................................................................
.........................................................................
.........................................................................
.........................................................................
.........................................................................
.........................................................................
.........................................................................
.........................................................................

*Attach photograph of project here*

# Craft Project

Name:

Date begun:

Date completed:

Who I made it for:

Inspiration or pattern source:

Materials used:

*Attach photograph of project here*

My notes:

# Craft Project

Name:
...................................................................

Date begun:
...................................................................

Date completed:
...................................................................

Who I made it for:
...................................................................

Inspiration or pattern source:
...................................................................
...................................................................

Materials used:
...................................................................
...................................................................
...................................................................
...................................................................
...................................................................
...................................................................
...................................................................

*Attach photograph of project here*

My notes:
...................................................................
...................................................................
...................................................................
...................................................................
...................................................................
...................................................................
...................................................................
...................................................................
...................................................................
...................................................................
...................................................................
...................................................................
...................................................................
...................................................................
...................................................................
...................................................................
...................................................................
...................................................................
...................................................................
...................................................................
...................................................................
...................................................................
...................................................................

# Craft Project

Name:
.....................................................................

Date begun:
.....................................................................

Date completed:
.....................................................................

Who I made it for:
.....................................................................

Inspiration or pattern source:
.....................................................................
.....................................................................

Materials used:
.....................................................................
.....................................................................
.....................................................................
.....................................................................
.....................................................................
.....................................................................
.....................................................................

*Attach photograph of project here*

My notes:
.....................................................................
.....................................................................
.....................................................................
.....................................................................
.....................................................................
.....................................................................
.....................................................................
.....................................................................
.....................................................................
.....................................................................
.....................................................................
.....................................................................
.....................................................................
.....................................................................
.....................................................................
.....................................................................
.....................................................................
.....................................................................
.....................................................................
.....................................................................
.....................................................................
.....................................................................
.....................................................................

# Craft Project

Name: ................................................

Date begun: ................................................

Date completed: ................................................

Who I made it for: ................................................

Inspiration or pattern source: ................................................

................................................

Materials used: ................................................

................................................

................................................

................................................

................................................

................................................

................................................

*Attach photograph of project here*

My notes: ................................................

................................................

................................................

................................................

................................................

................................................

................................................

................................................

................................................

................................................

................................................

................................................

................................................

................................................

................................................

................................................

................................................

................................................

................................................

................................................

................................................

................................................

................................................

................................................

................................................

# Craft Project

Name:
.......................................................

Date begun:
.......................................................

Date completed:
.......................................................

Who I made it for:
.......................................................

Inspiration or pattern source:
.......................................................
.......................................................

Materials used:
.......................................................
.......................................................
.......................................................
.......................................................
.......................................................
.......................................................
.......................................................
.......................................................

*Attach photograph of project here*

My notes:
.......................................................
.......................................................
.......................................................
.......................................................
.......................................................
.......................................................
.......................................................
.......................................................
.......................................................
.......................................................
.......................................................
.......................................................
.......................................................
.......................................................
.......................................................
.......................................................
.......................................................
.......................................................
.......................................................
.......................................................
.......................................................
.......................................................
.......................................................
.......................................................
.......................................................

# Craft Project

Name:

Date begun:

Date completed:

Who I made it for:

Inspiration or pattern source:

Materials used:

*Attach photograph of project here*

My notes:

# Craft Project

Name:
.................................................

Date begun:
.................................................

Date completed:
.................................................

Who I made it for:
.................................................

Inspiration or pattern source:
.................................................
.................................................

Materials used:
.................................................
.................................................
.................................................
.................................................
.................................................
.................................................
.................................................
.................................................
.................................................
.................................................

*Attach photograph of project here*

My notes:
.................................................
.................................................
.................................................
.................................................
.................................................
.................................................
.................................................
.................................................
.................................................
.................................................
.................................................
.................................................
.................................................
.................................................
.................................................
.................................................
.................................................
.................................................
.................................................
.................................................
.................................................
.................................................
.................................................
.................................................
.................................................
.................................................
.................................................
.................................................
.................................................
.................................................

# Craft Project

Name:

Date begun:

Date completed:

Who I made it for:

Inspiration or pattern source:

Materials used:

*Attach photograph of project here*

My notes:

# Craft Project

Name:
.....................................................

Date begun:
.....................................................

Date completed:
.....................................................

Who I made it for:
.....................................................

Inspiration or pattern source:
.....................................................
.....................................................

Materials used:
.....................................................
.....................................................
.....................................................
.....................................................
.....................................................
.....................................................
.....................................................
.....................................................

*Attach photograph of project here*

My notes:
.....................................................
.....................................................
.....................................................
.....................................................
.....................................................
.....................................................
.....................................................
.....................................................
.....................................................
.....................................................
.....................................................
.....................................................
.....................................................
.....................................................
.....................................................
.....................................................
.....................................................
.....................................................
.....................................................
.....................................................
.....................................................
.....................................................
.....................................................
.....................................................
.....................................................
.....................................................
.....................................................
.....................................................

# Craft Project

Name:
..............................................................

Date begun:
..............................................................

Date completed:
..............................................................

Who I made it for:
..............................................................

Inspiration or pattern source:
..............................................................
..............................................................

Materials used:
..............................................................
..............................................................
..............................................................
..............................................................
..............................................................
..............................................................
..............................................................

*Attach photograph of project here*

My notes:
..............................................................
..............................................................
..............................................................
..............................................................
..............................................................
..............................................................
..............................................................
..............................................................
..............................................................
..............................................................
..............................................................
..............................................................
..............................................................
..............................................................
..............................................................
..............................................................
..............................................................
..............................................................
..............................................................
..............................................................
..............................................................
..............................................................
..............................................................
..............................................................

# Craft Project

Name:

Date begun:

Date completed:

Who I made it for:

Inspiration or pattern source:

Materials used:

*Attach photograph of project here*

My notes:

# Craft Project

Name:

Date begun:

Date completed:

Who I made it for:

Inspiration or pattern source:

Materials used:

*Attach photograph of project here*

My notes:

# Craft Project

Name: ...................................

Date begun: ...........................

Date completed: .....................

Who I made it for: ..................

Inspiration or pattern source: ...

...........................................

Materials used: ......................

...........................................

...........................................

...........................................

...........................................

...........................................

...........................................

...........................................

*Attach photograph of project here*

My notes: ...............................

...........................................

...........................................

...........................................

...........................................

...........................................

...........................................

...........................................

...........................................

...........................................

...........................................

...........................................

...........................................

...........................................

...........................................

...........................................

...........................................

...........................................

...........................................

...........................................

...........................................

# Craft Project

Name:
.................................................

Date begun:
.................................................

Date completed:
.................................................

Who I made it for:
.................................................

Inspiration or pattern source:
.................................................
.................................................

Materials used:
.................................................
.................................................
.................................................
.................................................
.................................................
.................................................
.................................................
.................................................

*Attach photograph of project here*

My notes:
.................................................
.................................................
.................................................
.................................................
.................................................
.................................................
.................................................
.................................................
.................................................
.................................................
.................................................
.................................................
.................................................
.................................................
.................................................
.................................................
.................................................
.................................................
.................................................
.................................................
.................................................
.................................................
.................................................
.................................................

# Craft Project

Name:

Date begun:

Date completed:

Who I made it for:

Inspiration or pattern source:

Materials used:

*Attach photograph of project here*

My notes:

# Craft Project

Name: ..................................................

Date begun: ..........................................

Date completed: .....................................

Who I made it for: .................................

Inspiration or pattern source: .................
...............................................................

Materials used: .....................................
...............................................................
...............................................................
...............................................................
...............................................................
...............................................................
...............................................................
...............................................................

*Attach photograph of project here*

My notes: ...............................................
...............................................................
...............................................................
...............................................................
...............................................................
...............................................................
...............................................................
...............................................................
...............................................................
...............................................................
...............................................................
...............................................................
...............................................................
...............................................................
...............................................................
...............................................................
...............................................................
...............................................................
...............................................................
...............................................................
...............................................................
...............................................................
...............................................................
...............................................................
...............................................................

# Craft Project

Name:
.................................................

Date begun:
.................................................

Date completed:
.................................................

Who I made it for:
.................................................

Inspiration or pattern source:
.................................................
.................................................

Materials used:
.................................................
.................................................
.................................................
.................................................
.................................................
.................................................
.................................................

*Attach photograph of project here*

My notes:
.................................................
.................................................
.................................................
.................................................
.................................................
.................................................
.................................................
.................................................
.................................................
.................................................
.................................................
.................................................
.................................................
.................................................
.................................................
.................................................
.................................................
.................................................
.................................................
.................................................
.................................................
.................................................
.................................................
.................................................
.................................................

# Craft Project

Name:

Date begun:

Date completed:

Who I made it for:

Inspiration or pattern source:

Materials used:

*Attach photograph of project here*

My notes:

# Craft Project

Name:

Date begun:

Date completed:

Who I made it for:

Inspiration or pattern source:

Materials used:

Attach photograph of project here

My notes:

# Craft Project

Name:
.......................................................................

Date begun:
.......................................................................

Date completed:
.......................................................................

Who I made it for:
.......................................................................

Inspiration or pattern source:
.......................................................................
.......................................................................

Materials used:
.......................................................................
.......................................................................
.......................................................................
.......................................................................
.......................................................................
.......................................................................
.......................................................................

My notes:
.......................................................................
.......................................................................
.......................................................................
.......................................................................
.......................................................................
.......................................................................
.......................................................................
.......................................................................
.......................................................................
.......................................................................
.......................................................................
.......................................................................
.......................................................................
.......................................................................
.......................................................................
.......................................................................
.......................................................................
.......................................................................
.......................................................................
.......................................................................
.......................................................................
.......................................................................
.......................................................................

*Attach photograph of project here*

# Craft Project

Name: .........................................

Date begun: ...................................

Date completed: ...............................

Who I made it for: ............................

Inspiration or pattern source: ................

.............................................

Materials used:

.............................................

.............................................

.............................................

.............................................

.............................................

.............................................

.............................................

My notes: .....................................

.............................................

.............................................

.............................................

.............................................

.............................................

.............................................

.............................................

.............................................

.............................................

.............................................

.............................................

.............................................

.............................................

.............................................

.............................................

.............................................

.............................................

.............................................

.............................................

.............................................

*Attach photograph of project here*

# Craft Project

Name:
.................................................

Date begun:
.................................................

Date completed:
.................................................

Who I made it for:
.................................................

Inspiration or pattern source:
.................................................
.................................................

Materials used:
.................................................
.................................................
.................................................
.................................................
.................................................
.................................................
.................................................
.................................................

*Attach photograph of project here*

My notes:
.................................................
.................................................
.................................................
.................................................
.................................................
.................................................
.................................................
.................................................
.................................................
.................................................
.................................................
.................................................
.................................................
.................................................
.................................................
.................................................
.................................................
.................................................
.................................................
.................................................
.................................................
.................................................
.................................................
.................................................
.................................................
.................................................
.................................................
.................................................
.................................................
.................................................

# Craft Project

Name:

Date begun:

Date completed:

Who I made it for:

Inspiration or pattern source:

Materials used:

My notes:

*Attach photograph of project here*

# Craft Project

Name:
.................................................

Date begun:
.................................................

Date completed:
.................................................

Who I made it for:
.................................................

Inspiration or pattern source:
.................................................
.................................................

Materials used:
.................................................
.................................................
.................................................
.................................................
.................................................
.................................................
.................................................
.................................................
.................................................

*Attach photograph of project here*

My notes:
.................................................
.................................................
.................................................
.................................................
.................................................
.................................................
.................................................
.................................................
.................................................
.................................................
.................................................
.................................................
.................................................
.................................................
.................................................
.................................................
.................................................
.................................................
.................................................
.................................................
.................................................
.................................................
.................................................
.................................................
.................................................
.................................................

# Favorite Websites

# Notes

# Notes

# Notes

# Notes

# Notes

# Notes

# Notes

# Notes

# Notes

# Notes

# Notes

# Notes

# Notes

# Notes

# Notes

# Notes

# Notes

# Notes

# Notes

# Notes

# Notes

# Notes

# Notes

# Notes

# Notes

# Notes

# Notes

# Notes

GEORGE SHERIDAN KNOWLES (1863-1931)
*The Sleighride*
PRIVATE COLLECTION / FINE ART PHOTOGRAPHIC LIBRARY, LONDON

PUBLISHED BY PAVILION BOOKS LIMITED